Out of Darkness,
Into the Marvelous Light

Out of Darkness,
Into the Marvelous Light

VERONICA
RILEY

To purchase books in bulk or for additional information, contact the publisher.

Mynd Matters Publishing
2690 Cobb Pkwy SE, Ste A5-375, Smyrna, GA 30080
www.myndmatterspublishing.com

978-1-963874-59-4 (pbk)
978-1-963874-60-0 (hdcv)
978-1-963874-61-7 (ebook)

FIRST EDITION

To my two beautiful daughters, Natasha and Dametreea, who I love and cherish with all my heart. I call them my Soaring Eagle, and my Beautiful Butterfly. They have always been there for me through the good, the bad, and the ugly. They both always had encouraging words to download into my broken spirit. I thank God that He allowed me to give birth to two wonderful daughters. They have truly been angels in my life. They are my heroes.

I Love You Much!
#SuperMom

Contents

Out of Darkness,
Into the Marvelous Light

Preface

Domestic abuse, also known as intimate partner violence (IPV) affects more than 12 million people each year. It was, and continues to be, widespread in our society, with one in three women and one in four men having experienced some form of domestic abuse in their lifetime. While these statistics are startling, consider that many cases of abuse go unreported, so the numbers are much higher. As someone who understands the experiences that exist within those statistics, I knew I had to write a book to help other women, young and old, by shedding some light on the signs and structures of abuse. Signs we may subconsciously ignore, because we aren't taught to look for hidden and harmful things when dating and finding a romantic partner.

Before we continue, I want to make one thing clear: I don't believe all men are abusive. There are some real men out there who will treat you like a precious jewel, appreciate who you are as a person, passionately love you, and never lay a hand on you except to caress and hold you. I appreciate and acknowledge those men.

I wrote *Out of Darkness, Into the Marvelous Light* to help women who may find themselves needing to read these words find the strength and courage to walk away, and to reinforce the truth that there is always light at the end of even the darkest of tunnels. It is also for those who may be wondering if they are already seeing signals that warn of a much more troubling future.

We were not created by God to live any part of our lives being verbally, mentally, and/or physically abused. My prayer is that this book will help other women avoid going through what I experienced and help the women who are already in their nightmare find a safe way out. We are worthy of every good thing that life has to offer us. We do not have to settle, and we should never want to.

INTRODUCTION

How long will we as women continue to find ourselves in the same old rut? Situations where we have been dumped on by a spouse or significant other, who abused us, used us, and then kicked us to the curb because they no longer have any use for us? Our ancestors, grandmothers, mothers, aunts, sisters, and daughters have suffered and currently suffer at the words and hands of their abusers. Women of all ages are being murdered because they want out of their abusive situations, so they try to leave or divorce their abuser, which in many cases ends fatally because the abuser's warped way of thinking is, *if I can't have you, no one will.*

Now, if a woman happens to survive an abusive relationship, she is usually left at the bottom of a pit—a deep, dark hole that she may attempt to crawl out of only to find that when she finally reaches the top, she's too weak or afraid to pull herself completely out. She's in a rut.

A rut is a fixed or established mode of procedure, or course of life, usually dull or unpromising. The Oxford Dictionary defines a rut as:

> *A habit or pattern of behavior that has become*
> *dull and unproductive but is hard to change.*

There is nothing good about being in a rut, nothing at all. For those of us who make it out, we tend to spend our entire adult lives recovering from what I call the dark side. Why? After you have allowed yourself to enter or travel into an abusive relationship, you find yourself in an unfamiliar place, so you continue to travel through the situation, believing things will get better. However, things do not get better. You then continue the journey, holding on to what little hope remains, still believing it *will get better*. While you search for better, you stumble upon a landmine, which is full of danger zones, and now it is too late, the battle has begun.

I use the term rut because some of us are repeat offenders. We run from one abuser right into the arms of another and don't understand why. One reason why we continue to repeat the "offense" is that we do not yield or even come to a stop when something that should set off the safety alarm is said to us. We do not give it a second thought, and we tend to let it go over our heads because we are still in the process of "getting to know each other." When something is said nonchalantly, we also receive it nonchalantly. We receive the statements just as passively as they were made. In a nutshell, we ignore the first warning sign. Not only do we need to have our eyes open so we can physically see which way the relationship is going, but we need to have our ears tuned into what is being said and the way it is being said. We all have an inner voice or an inner feeling that rises inside of us when something is not quite right. I personally ignored that voice and the feeling many times, and because I did not heed to the warning signs, I suffered greatly. Throughout the on-and-off ordeal of my past relationship, I found myself asking this question: *When is enough, enough, and how do I safely get out of this situation?*

I'm sure many women have asked themselves

this same question. The sad truth is many women never make it out. They end up dying at the hands of their abuser—the very person who vowed to love and honor them till death, but the only thing abusers seem to honor is the till death part. In their minds, you only have two choices: do or die. This means his way or no way at all.

Back in the day, abuse was hidden in the home. What went on between those four walls usually stayed inside those four walls. The women would not utter a word about it. Therefore, no one outside of the home knew what they were going through. It was a family secret. Even the children kept quiet because they were too afraid to say anything. Abused women were careful to hide the bruises on their bodies and were afraid to take a stand to speak out against what was going on inside their homes. This became a way of life until the end of their life. Now, abuse has traveled outside of the home because the abuser doesn't care about who is watching anymore. Some abusers chase women down streets with weapons, make public threats, and physically assault them without a concern for who may see.

Many women today are overwhelmed with so much fear inside, fear of the so-called man of the house, whom everyone in the house is trained to fear. This inherent, but still learned, fear was nine times out of ten how the man of the house was raised to run his house. It had always been done this way, passed down from generation to generation. It is like a never-ending story because the children in the home who sit on the sidelines and watch this horrible thing happen, soak it all in, and take it into the next generation. Abuse is a sick and reckless behavior, and it frequently leaves behind nothing more than grief, chaos, and death.

CHAPTER ONE

IN THE BEGINNING

Then the Lord God formed a man from the dust of the ground and breathed into his nostrils the breath of life, and the man became a living being. Now the Lord God had planted a garden in the east, in Eden; and there He put the man He had formed. And the Lord God made all kinds of trees grow out of the ground - trees that were pleasing to the eye and good for food. In the middle of the Garden were the tree of life and the tree of the knowledge of good and evil. The Lord God took the man and put him in the Garden of Eden to work it and take care of it.

And the Lord God commanded the man, "You are free to eat from any tree in the garden; but you must not eat from the tree of the knowledge of good and evil, for when you eat of it you will surely die."

The Lord God said, "It is not good for the man to be alone. I will make a helper suitable for him." So, the Lord God caused the man to fall into a deep sleep; and while he was sleeping, He took one of the man's ribs and closed the place with flesh. Then the Lord God made a woman from the rib He had taken out of the man, and He brought her to the man.

The man said, "This is now bone of my bones and flesh of my flesh; she shall be called 'woman,' for she was taken out of man." Adam and his wife were both naked, and they felt no shame. Adam named his wife Eve, because she would become the mother of all the living.

Gen 2:7-9, 2:15-18, 2:21-23, 2:25, 3:20

Eve means *Life*. When I read these verses, it blew me away because women literally came out of man. God opened Adam up, took a rib, and created a woman. God could have chosen another way to create women. He could have formed her the way He did Adam, from the dust of the ground, or He could have just spoken her into existence. God specifically chose to take her out of man and present her back to man. Eve was a gift from God, made especially for Adam. God made her as Adam put it, "Bone of my Bones, and Flesh of my Flesh" *(Gen 2:23 NIV)*. Eve was Adam's soulmate to love, honor, and cherish for life. Adam and Eve had the perfect relationship. Nothing was out of order in the garden. It was a beautiful, peaceful place, which is like getting married for the first time or entering a brand-new relationship. The wedding atmosphere is so refreshing, so alive. You feel wanted and loved. It feels like the perfect relationship—like Adam and Eve, nothing is out of order. It remained that way until the serpent entered the garden and deceived Eve with words that were not God's truth.

In Eve's case, all it took was for her to have a casual conversation with the enemy, who was disguised as a serpent. Now the serpent was craftier than any of the wild animals the Lord God had made *(Gen 3:1 NIV)*. Satan tricked Eve into doing something God told her not to do by planting a bad seed in her mind when he said to her, "Did God really say, you must not eat from any tree in the garden?" Eve went on to say, "We may eat fruit from the trees in the garden, but God did say, 'You must not eat fruit from the tree that is in the middle of the garden, and you must not touch it, or you will die."

The serpent said to Eve, "You will not certainly die. For God knows that when you eat of it your eyes will be opened, and you will be like God, knowing good and evil." When the woman saw that the fruit of the tree was good for food and pleasing to the eye, and desirable for gaining wisdom, she took some and ate it. (*Gen 3:1- 3:6, NIV*).

God told Eve not to eat from a certain tree in the garden, but she went against what He told her and suffered great consequences. Not only did she make life hard for herself, but she also made life hard for Adam. Keep in mind that God verbally gave Adam and Eve specific instructions. This wasn't an inside voice that God downloaded into her spirit, and if He had done it that way, there was still no excuse for Eve to ignore it.

When women ignore the voice of God, I call it the Eve Syndrome. When we meet or notice a man, we tend to look at the tree—what it looks like, weak or strong, and then we take a glance at its fruit, his looks, and whether he is desirable and pleasing to the eye. Although he has not approached yet, something starts to rise inside the woman that makes her want more.

Sometimes we need to take a step back and

analyze what we see. Take a deeper look and allow God to intervene. There have been times in my life when I looked at a man and got an uncomfortable feeling. When that feeling comes upon you, that is your first warning sign. A stop sign should immediately go up. There should be no reason for you to carry on any conversation with this person. The feeling that rose in you did so for a reason. Despite what God told Eve to do, she still took it upon herself to have a conversation with the enemy. If the spirit of God dwells inside of you, you have a built-in alarm system that will never fail. All you need to do is acknowledge it and stop ignoring it. You cannot afford to keep moving forward when the Holy Spirit is telling you not to venture down that path. God knows what is best for you. He is looking out for your best interest. The mistake Eve and Adam made, choosing to eat from that one forbidden tree, destroyed everything they had. In many relationships, the enemy has planted the seed of abuse. The abuser's job is the same as the serpent's job in the garden—to kill, steal, and destroy.

It is time to stop the madness before it even begins. We are a *gift* to man. We are precious and priceless gifts, taken out of man, and given back to man, to love, honor, and cherish. Not to beat, break, and destroy. Abuse, whether verbal or physical, is destructive. It is inhumane. It imprisons too many women in their own homes and in their own minds because of the fear they live with, along with the fear of the enemy with which they dwell.

Before I continue, I want to again stress that not all men are abusive. There are many men who will never raise a hand to physically or verbally abuse a woman. I have heard repeatedly that hurt people hurt people. There are so many men who have been hurt in the past as children, teenagers, and even as adults, and they may not know how to deal with whatever has been done to them. They may not know how to recover from what they have experienced living in an abusive home.

When abuse is ignored, and the abuser(s) and those abused are unable to get the help they need, due to pride, circumstances, or the inability to confront internal demons, the hurt and consequences of their experience are buried deep inside and often show up in toxic and unhealthy ways. It's akin to having a ticking time bomb buried inside, ready to go off at any moment. When, where, and who will experience the explosion is not always known.

Ladies, it is time to get serious. It is no longer an option to put up with anything and everything just to say we have a man in our lives. When you put up with anything and accept everything a man throws your way, you can be sure that he will push every limit and disregard all boundaries. Satan wants you to believe this is the only kind of man you can attract because he knows you will look past all the signs of abuse. Believe me, the signs are there, but we sometimes choose to put them on the back burner where the flame is low. We tend to think that because the flame is low, things are not *that bad right now*. Because the relationship is still early, we ignore little sarcastic and belittling comments. We ignore them because we are in the "intrigue" stage of the relationship. However, we must begin to discern the signs of an evil spirit. Some men are just like Satan, crafty and cunning, and will lure you in through trickery. These types of men are pros at what they do. They will tell you what you want to hear, and some of us soak it all in like a sponge without giving the sincerity of their words a second thought.

Finding yourself in an abusive relationship will destroy the mind, body, and soul, and is a slow, agonizing death. I know because I've lived this story, and I am a survivor, by the grace of God. What is interesting is that an abuser will tell you he cannot live without you. I perceived it this way: he could not live without me as a living, breathing being, but he seemed just fine to be on the verge of putting me six feet under. Abusive men have no problem slithering off to find the next victim to destroy. Abuse is all about transforming you into what he wants you to be and where he allows you to go.

CHAPTER TWO

POWER AND CONTROL

A "power trip" is defined as an activity or way of behaving that makes a person feel powerful; something that a person does for the pleasure of using power to control other people. Meaning, power and control operate hand-in-hand.

Once an abusive man knows he has the power to control you, he will. You may as well be a robot, with him holding the remote control and changing the channel (rules) any time he feels like it.

Let's look at how abusers differ. In some cases, the abuse starts immediately. While in others, it happens over time. The process may be slower in some instances because it takes time to gain power and control over a strong-willed woman. The abuser must win you over first, which makes him work overtime to get you where he wants you. Eventually, once he knows your vulnerabilities and has created an emotional connection with you, things will begin to change. He will start to change with the aim of breaking you down.

When an abuser has conquered your heart, the next victory for him is your mind. You begin to see a side of him you have never seen before. Suddenly, the kind words from him stop. The hugging and caressing stop. The loving words stop, along with the flowers and little gifts he used to shower you with. His former words and actions are replaced by threats, a foul and vicious tongue, and hurtful fists. His degrading words that you never knew existed are now being poured over you like a running faucet to make you feel small and worthless. Your world has just been crushed and now resides in his sick, pathetic world. You put up with it because fear has set in, and you do not know which way to turn. You do not know how to get out of it and you do not know who to tell because you do not know who you can trust to keep your big secret from getting back to your abuser. Over time, you find yourself stuck between a rock and a hard place with no way out. You cannot move forward. You cannot move at all. It is as if you fell into quicksand, and the more you struggle to get yourself out, the faster you sink.

You find yourself giving up, being still, and quiet about the entire situation. You are slowly dying on the inside and putting up a front on the outside for the world to see because you do not want anyone you know and care about to discover this dark world you live in at home. Another reason for cutting yourself off from the outside world is being embarrassed about the situation you have gotten yourself into. You are embarrassed about not being strong enough to take a stand against your abuser because the fear of him is so deeply embedded inside of your being.

With all this happening, we become withdrawn, we totally lay our self-esteem down on the floor, and we surrender to this horrible, ungodly situation. We no longer see the light at the end of the tunnel. Because of fear, we choose to dwell in darkness for years because we do not know how to face our fears.

The relationship I had with my abuser remained the same. The only thing that changed is that I decided to bring innocent children into my nightmare. Not only did I have to worry about my safety, but I also had to worry about the safety of my two daughters. It is never okay to bring children into an unsafe environment, but I did, and I lived to regret it. I made the situation I was in even more impossible to get out of. When I chose to have children with him, it escalated my fear of him because he chose to use our children as a weapon to keep me in line and to keep me from leaving him. As women, we tend to "fall in line" because our children mean the world to us.

I remember living in an apartment complex on the east side of town. We had some kind of falling out as usual, and after the drama was over, he left. At least I thought he left. I was upset and tired of it being the same mess, just a different day, so I picked up my baby and headed out the door. When I got almost halfway down the stairs, I ran into him coming up the stairs. There were some words exchanged, and he reached out to take my baby right out of my arms. I hesitated to give my child up, but I knew if I started anything, it would end up pretty bad. I also knew I did not want to go out in public, yelling and playing a tug-of-war game with my baby being pulled to and from. I let go of her. He turned and walked away with my baby and there was nothing I could do.

I cannot begin to explain the pain that set deep inside of me, watching him walk away with the one thing that brought me joy during the nightmare I lived in. I did not know when or if he would bring her back to me, and the sick thing about it all was as he turned to walk away, he had a smile on his face. He knew he had the upper hand, and he knew I would be in torment until he decided to bring my baby back to me. The smile on his face signified to him that he held all power in his hands. Fear kept me from fighting back. I was in bondage to fear. It was a constant yoke around my neck and chains that bound my feet.

Children should never have to grow up in such an environment. Day in and day out, many children stand on the sidelines and watch their mothers being tormented by the father figure in the house. Over the years, as they continue to watch, another seed is being planted, nourished, and starts growing. On the sidelines, the boys are learning how to manipulate and torment, while the girls are learning to fear and submit to their abusers. This is an unhealthy environment for children, and down the line, if not consciously addressed with healthy tools and methods, it will affect them in a myriad of negative ways. With each generation abuse enters, the impact becomes more powerful than the generation it came out of. Domestic violence and the number of deaths because of it are increasing. Why? Because we ignore details. We overlook the warning signs, and before we know it, it is too late, and the abuser has gained the upper hand in the relationship.

The abuser (the enemy) wants the same thing Satan (the enemy) wants—to take you to this deep, dark bottomless pit to live in pain, agony, and be tormented because he has never let go of the pain, agony, and torment that lives inside of him. He wants your mind, body, and soul. The enemy is not who our souls belong to. The enemy did not breathe the breath of life into us, but is more than willing to take it away from us.

This is how much power we allow them to have, and that is too much power for any man to hold in his hands. It is urgent that we stop giving men such power and control over our lives because an abuser is going to use it for his own advantage. He is going to use it in sinful, evil ways. An evil person does not care about your well-being or the children's well-being either. Please don't mistake me, I understand why it is so hard to tear yourself away from the hell you live in, especially when there are kids involved. In my case, the reason I stayed in and out of my horrible relationship was because I wanted to have a forever relationship, a "till-death-do-you-part marriage" with the man I chose to marry. I wanted our children to be raised in a two-parent home because that was rare in the neighborhoods where I grew up. It was also rare in my childhood home. I believed in one marriage for a lifetime. I knew for sure that I was not going to be in and out of different marriages, and I wanted my children to have the same father because this was also rare where I grew up. All of this was very important to me.

Before I met the man who later became my abuser and spouse, I lived in San Diego, California, until my stepdad got military orders to move to Tucson, Arizona. My mother, stepdad, siblings, and I arrived in Tucson in 1977. It was a horrible place to live and the school we attended was rampant with violence. I hated living in Tucson and held resentment in my heart towards my mom and stepdad for moving our family there. I was bussed to Tucson High School from the military base where we lived. Tucson High School is where I met my ex-husband. He did not attend the school. He just showed up on campus one day with some friends.

We dated for several years before we got married.

I went against everything I believed in. My morals and values, along with my self-esteem, went out the window. I finished high school and briefly attended Pima Community College, but for some reason, college did not work out for me. My dream was simple: have a nice office job, meet the man of my dreams, get married, and have four beautiful children—two boys and two girls—and live happily ever after. I had a simple plan until I met and fell in love with my abuser.

As we continued to date, and as I began to settle for less, all my plans and dreams, along with my morals and values, began to fade away. Why? Because my abuser had plans of his own.

Now let's break down the plan I settled for. First, I dated him way too long because he was not ready to get married. I continued to date him even though I saw signs of abuse. I ignored the fact that it bothered me, and I was a little fearful of him when he got angry.

Second, I wanted to have children, and since marriage was not in the picture anytime soon, I ventured farther away from my values. I agreed to have children out of wedlock. I believe this is called "stuck on stupid."

Third, I moved in with him while he was still

living with his mother. This is also one of the things that I greatly regret because we were not married, and I see it as highly disrespectful.

The abuse escalated into an unimaginable nightmare, but I stayed because fear had me bound, and I was still holding on to my forever dream. I was young, inexperienced, and worst of all, didn't have a relationship with God. Therefore, I didn't know how to spot the warning signs, and because I didn't know what to look for, I fell into the hands of the enemy. I allowed the enemy to come in and rob me of many years of my life. These were years of ups and downs, ins and outs, and physical, emotional, and mental hurts and pains. He fathered children with other women while we were dating *and* during our marriage. I almost let it take me out.

This was not God's plan for my life. This was the enemy's plan and I fell for it. If it had not been for the Lord walking silently by my side, I would not have made it out alive. Even though God was there, I could not feel His presence. I did not know He was there with me through it all. I know now, without a shadow of doubt, that He was there. He went through it all with me. He was waiting for me to meet Him halfway. I had to get to a point of truly being sick and tired of being sick and tired, and finally ready to step out on faith. I had to step out regardless of my fears and trust God to get me out of the grave I'd dug for myself. There were times I did not know for sure if I was going to make it out, and the only reason I did is because during my weakest moments, God gave me the strength I needed to continue.

It is time out for women dying at the hands of their significant others. It is time out for being weak and afraid. It is really time out for going back and forth with yourself on whether to hang in there a little longer because maybe someday, at some point, he will see the light and change his ways. Keep in mind that for many women, someday never comes.

During the storm I was going through, I often asked myself, *When will it all end? When will I be able to turn on the TV and not hear or see news or movies about women being beaten, shot, strangled, dismembered, or stabbed to death?* It grieves my spirit to sit and watch things like this. It also makes me angry because the memories from my private hell begin to resurface, and then the tears start to flow. It all takes me back to a place I do not want to revisit. Those wounds from my past are too difficult to revisit and have not completely healed. For this reason, I believe we should avoid anything that may hinder or trigger us in any way. Now I try to focus on wholesome, spirit-filled movies that are nurturing to my soul. Before I had a starring role in my own domestic violence drama, I had no problem watching movies about abuse. I used to sit and judge the women and call them stupid for putting up with it. I made sarcastic comments like, *I wish a man would do that to me*, or *if a man did that to me, I would do this or I would do that.* I did not understand why the women in the movies would not just walk away from their situations. I did not get it, until one day I was in their shoes. The very thing I told myself I would never let happen came knocking on my door. It never entered the back or front of my mind that the person I chose to spend the rest of my life with would explode and become the violent and evil person that he became. I began questioning myself, *How did I miss the signs? How did I not see it coming?* We do not see it coming because love tends to blind us from the reality of bad situations.

Love will make you put things on the back burner, and a back burner unattended can lead to dangerous and fatal situations. You should never ignore any sign of abuse, especially the small, discrete ones.

CHAPTER THREE

THE EXAMINATION

As women, we look for everything we want in a man and ignore the warning signs of abuse. When we are hanging out with the girls, we almost always find ourselves on the topic of men. We talk about what kind of man we are attracted to and how we would like our perfect man to be. It is as if we are looking at a build-your-own-man menu.

The first thing on the menu is looks. He has to look good and be "fine." I call this the appetizer. It is what we look at first. We cannot seem to make up our minds about what type of man we want to start with because everything looks pleasing to the eye. Further down on the menu, we come to the main course. He must have a body and a half. We tend to spend a little more time checking him out. The meat represents the body. That is what we look at first when our plate arrives. We check to make sure it is just how we want it to be. The "and a half" represents all the accompanying side dishes—the extras that make everything come together for the perfect meal/perfect man.

After we have exhausted ourselves on the main course, we ask for a doggy bag or a to-go container. This represents everything we ignored or did not finish. We take it home, put it in the fridge, and sometimes forget it is there. When we finally get back to it, it is too late. It is no good, ruined, and ends up in the trash.

Now let's get back to the menu. A meal is not complete without dessert. This is something most of us cannot do without. It completes the meal. It is the glitter and icing on the cake. It is something we do not really need but prefer to have. This represents the material things that a man may possess, such as a luxury car, money, designer clothes, etc.

There is nothing wrong with the glitter, but keep in mind that not everything that glitters is always what it seems to be. There could be a high price you end up paying for running after the shine. Sometimes, it is just another distraction to keep you from recognizing the enemy. Be very careful about seeking the glitter, for it is not a necessity, and the glitter is only temporary.

> *"Do not store up for yourselves [material] treasures on earth. But store up for yourselves treasures in heaven. For where your treasure is, there your heart [your wishes, your desires; that on which your life centers] will be also.*
> *—Matthew 6:19-21 (AMP Bible)*

Instead of focusing on the exterior, we should prioritize what exists on the inside. Pray and ask God to help you look beyond what is on the outside so you can see the person's true intentions. The Holy Spirit will never let you down and will never lead you in the wrong direction. Below are some lifesaving questions that should be addressed on your first date. Doing so in person also allows you to be watchful of his reactions and see if he gets agitated in any way. If he does get agitated, you'll have your first red flag. If his intentions toward you are good, you should be able to inquire about anything without any negative reaction from him.

- *Where was he born and raised?*
- *What is his family background?*

- *What kind of relationship did/does he have with his parents and siblings?*

- *What has been his journey since leaving his parents' home? (Note: ensure he does not still live with his parent(s))*

- *What are his present and future plans?*

- *What are his morals and values?*

- *Has he ever been in a long-term relationship, and if so, what happened that brought the relationship to an end?*

- *Has he ever been a victim of abuse?*

Make sure you're on the lookout for signs of deception. If he is a Dr. Jekyll/Mr. Hyde, he will keep the most dangerous things about himself hidden. Often, questions like these do not even begin to enter our minds until it is too late. We automatically think everyone we meet is generally a good person. The truth is, you see only the "good" side someone will present to you, but it's important to look closer because life or death and peace of mind depend on how deep your examination goes.

Let the examination begin. Examination is the act or process of carefully looking at someone or something to learn about its condition or to discover facts. The only way you can find out what that missing something is, is to become a private investigator. The keyword is to investigate, discreetly, of course. Leverage technology to get all the information you need.

As you search, keep in mind that the one thing you are looking for is any kind of violent act. In some cases, it may not appear right away, so you will have to call on the Holy Spirit to bless you with the gift of discernment. Discernment is the ability to properly judge a situation through the Holy Spirit's provided wisdom and understanding. This is your internal alarm that will help guide you and allow you to see a man's true intentions. Discernment is a must-have for you to live an uncompromising, abuse-free life.

Dear friends, do not believe every spirit, but test the spirit to see whether they are from God, because many false prophets have gone out into the world.

—1 John 4:1 (NIV)

Meet and Greet. Typically, the initial meeting between a man and a woman includes a greeting, an exchange of names, and some basic conversation. Then, if everything is to your satisfaction and there appears to be potential, you exchange phone numbers. Whether you meet that day or at some point soon, your thoughts begin to consume you after the interaction. For the rest of the day, you might think about the brief time you spent talking with him. With a smile on your face, you anticipate his phone call or hearing his voice. You continue to communicate until finally, you are on your way to a real date.

While on the date, you can talk even more, which is your opportunity to really get to know the man. You cannot afford to be afraid to ask him personal questions, and do not put it off for a more *appropriate* time because there is no more appropriate time. You need to learn as much as you possibly can about him, as fast as you can. During that date and any conversation, be conscious of every word that comes out of his mouth. Be aware of the way he reacts during small, senseless, playful disagreements. Like when you are debating over where to eat, or when you are discussing a movie you both went to see, but have differing opinions on it. I know from experience that something as simple as a difference of opinion can lead to a violent act. Please keep in mind that in the abuser's mind, he is always right and you'd better see things exactly as he sees them. I eventually learned to keep my personal opinions to myself at times, while at other times, I felt like I needed to be heard. The times I chose to speak up were because I do have a mind of my own, and a God-given right to voice my opinion on any subject I want. With that said, no man at any given time, disagreement or not, has the right to put his hands on you. Man is not our Creator, and he definitely did not breathe the breath of life into our lungs. Ladies, we are fearfully and wonderfully made by God (Psalm 139:14 NIV). As my sister would say, "That's it, that's all." Now, let's look at some very important "red flags."

CHAPTER FOUR

THE WARNING SIGNS

The Tongue (Verbal Abuse)

The tongue has the power of life and death, and those who love it will eat its fruit *(Proverbs 18:21 NIV)*. On judgment day everyone will be held accountable for every harsh and careless word that came out of their mouths.

When we put bits into the mouths of horses to make them obey us, we can turn the whole animal. Or take ships as an example, although they are large and driven by strong winds, they are steered by a very small rudder. Likewise, the tongue is a small part of the body, but it makes great boasts. Consider how a massive forest can be set ablaze by a small spark. The tongue is also a fire, a world of evil among the parts of the body. It can corrupt the whole person, set the course of one's life on fire, and is itself set on fire by hell. But no man can tame the tongue. It is a restless evil, full of deadly poison (*James 3:3-6, 8 NIV*).

Verbal abuse is the most important warning sign of them all. The tongue is a powerful weapon. It's referred to as a weapon because if the wrong words are constantly being downloaded into your mind and into your spirit, those words will affect your heart and eventually destroy the positive spirit dwelling within you. The wrong words can leave you feeling like you have been cut by a knife and the bleeding starts deep within the flesh, deep down where your soul lies, and little by little, the knife is pushed deeper and deeper with every belittling word that is uttered from the lips of someone who says they love you.

Throughout the many, many years I spent in the darkness of abuse, I would remember what was said to me more than what was done to me. The statement I struggled to shake off was when he told me I was a thorn in his side. Think about that for a minute. Can you imagine how painful it would be to have a thorn stuck in your side? My mind went deeper into what he said to me because I have been pricked by the thorns on a rose many times. A thorn is very sharp, and depending on how deep it goes into your finger, it can also cause bleeding. The pain can last for days.

I could not comprehend how he could utter such hurtful and harmful words to me. I could not shake off what he said to me. His words burrowed deep inside my soul, and I did not know how to ease the hurt to quiet the echoes. That night when I went to bed, I turned over onto my side and cried. Words impact us more than we know. The wrong words spoken, especially out of anger, can cause you to have a mental breakdown, and at some point, you start to believe you are what the abuser says you are.

It is extremely important to pay close attention to what is said and how it is said. Listen for the tone of voice change when you are conversing with one another. Teach yourself how to zero in on particular words that co-exist with the voice change. In the typical situation, the words coming from an abuser's mouth may not be harsh at first—unnoticeable—so we let them go over our heads and down the backside. We think nothing of it. A little sarcastic put down here, a sarcastic put down there, and before you know it, the situation has gotten totally out of control. You are being called every bad name in the book. Your real name no longer exists. You are now confused and wondering, *How in the world did I allow the relationship to get to this level?* It got to that level because you ignored the warning signs.

Verbal abuse is like a snake. It slithers into a conversation, unannounced, and when the timing is right, it launches out and strikes you. It downloads venom into your being and all is downhill from there. The venom an abuser uses is words that weaken your mind and spirit. During this period in my past relationship, I was dealing with physical and verbal abuse.

I was literally a nervous wreck. I was withdrawn from my family and friends, not by choice, but because the fear of him that dwelled within me gave him the power to pick and choose which family and/or friends were allowed over to see me. When you start to fear someone, you become afraid to be your true self. You become afraid to speak up and defend yourself because the light that used to dwell inside of you has become a dark and void place. When I reached my void place, I gave myself a pity party. I thought of myself as a worthless human being. Every time I looked in the mirror, I saw a weak, pitiful, ugly person. I hated myself, and I turned against myself. I became my own worst enemy because I allowed a man to input bad, filthy, and degrading things inside of my being. At that point I did not know how to get unstuck. So, for a season, I stopped defending myself. I gave up. I learned to be silent. Instead of doing tit-for-tat, I just listened. I became like a sponge. I absorbed and downloaded every hurtful word into my mind, heart, and soul.

After a while, only a part of me would listen to him and the other part would try to block it out. I tried to go somewhere else in my mind. This was an exercise I used to do to hurt less and bleed a little less inside while I was being verbally torn down. I believe that every negative word that comes out of the abuser's mouth is coming from his heart, to rip away at your heart, so you can feel exactly how he is feeling. He is in pain, and he refuses to be in pain all by himself. No matter what you say to try and calm the anger that is raging inside of him, he refuses to be comforted. As a result, I often remained silent and allowed him to get to the end of his tantrum.

Abuse starts with words, and fear rises from words. That's why I say again to pay close attention to his words, actions, and reactions. Notice things that may be "cute" in the beginning but send up a caution flag. Trust me, subtle craziness is always revealed, but most of the time, ignored. When fear starts to creep in, do not question it. Instead, do a 180-degree turn and get yourself back into the light of life.

Trust

While you were dating and before things got serious, he did not mind you spending time with family and friends. You basically told him about your plans and the reply was a simple, "Ok, have a good time" or "I'll see you when you get back." After some time passes, he suddenly becomes Inspector Gadget. The words, "Ok, have a good time," or "I'll see you later," get replaced with, "Where are you going? Who are you going with or meeting up with? How many people will be there? What time will you be back?" Again, we tend to think this is cute and miss the signs, which is exactly what he wants. He wants it to go over your head because he knows you are not paying attention to the warnings he is throwing your way. Eventually, you become a little agitated because you are tired of being interrogated every time you want to walk out the door. However, the leaving interrogation does not compare to the coming home interrogation, especially when you are not back at home at the time you told him you would be back.

When you walk through the door, there he is waiting for you, and nine times out of ten, it is not because he missed you. Be careful because he is in what I refer to as the "Yellow Zone." The first thing you need to be aware of is the tone of voice change—angry but subtle. Does he start to make accusations that you were not where you said you would be? This is where you need to be cautious. He is already trippin' so do not make matters worse. This is not the time for a word-for-word battle because he has already made up his mind and is ready to escalate to the next level, which is the "Red Zone." He is looking for a reason to put his hands on you. The wrong word, posture, or facial expression from you will get him up out of his chair and before you know it, damage has been done. It was a no-win situation the moment you walked through the door. He is not interested in anything you have to say because while he was waiting for you to get home, he filled his own head with a bunch of lies. The only thing to do in a situation like this is to de-escalate. Proceed with caution and beat him at his own game. Nothing is worth him hurting you in any way. To avoid drama, simply apologize and explain the reason why you are running behind. Attitude is not the way to go. If this method happens to work, then you have survived the first round. There will be many more to come, this I know for sure. This warning sign is not going away. It is only going to get worse as time passes, and the outcome next time will elevate as well. Approaching an abuser in the wrong way could land you in the hospital or an early grave. My personal advice is to find a safe place for you and your children to go to ASAP. Make sure it is not the home of your relatives or friends, as that will be the first place the abuser will call or head to. Make sure it is a haven that no one knows about. There are many private domestic violence centers that you can reach out to for help. Please don't wait until it's too late.

Possessiveness

This is something you will not recognize at first because when your man wants you to spend more time with him, that makes you feel good. However, at some point, it becomes a problem when you must leave him to spend time with family and friends. Therefore, he slowly begins to fill up his calendar with "couples" things to do. You will slowly begin to lessen and/or erase things to do from your own calendar. The thing is, you really will not have a clue of what is going on, but at some point, your friends and family start to notice you do not have time to hang out with them like you used to. Eventually, you will get a phone call, basically inquiring about what is going on with you. Because you still do not have a clue, you may say something like, "I've been busy and I don't really have time anymore," or "My man wants us to spend more quality time together." The reality is that he does not want to spend more time with you. He wants to take your time away from everyone else. He does not want to share you with anyone, and he wants your undivided attention, 24/7. This is not a healthy relationship because he is putting you in a box that has a knob in the back, and he wants to be the controller. He is literally taking your freedom away, and women in general have fought too hard for freedom in this world to let some man come along and take it away. If your spouse or boyfriend really loves and cares about you, then he will care about you having a well-balanced and healthy lifestyle outside of the home.

Pay attention to how things are shifting in your relationship and pay attention to how things are shrinking outside of your relationship. The abuser's plan is to make sure he removes everyone who is taking your time away from him. After he has accomplished that, ownership sets in. This means you are no longer equal partners. He has elevated his role and downsized yours. He now sees you as something he owns. Someone he looks down on. It is like you are not even human anymore. You have become a piece of property...some land that he invested in and he has to work it, break it in, and build it into exactly what he wants it to be. Know that he will not rest until this task is done. This is an inhumane thing to do to someone you claim to love. The one thing I know for sure is that the only person I owe myself to is Jesus Christ. He is the only one who paid the price for me. He was beaten and bruised for me. He suffered all the way to Calvary for me. He hung on the cross for me. He shed his blood for me. He is the only one I truly belong to. He is my owner. My abuser is not. He did not do any of these things for me. He sacrificed absolutely nothing for me. In my past, in the home with my abuser, I took the hits, and I shed the blood.

When abuse enters a relationship, you become fearful, not really understanding the depth of what you've entered. Once again, it is because you looked over or ignored very important red flags. Because you are trying to make sense out of the madness, you start to make up excuses for him being the way he is. *Maybe he's just having a bad day. Maybe it's me. What am I not doing right?*

It's not about you. It's about the abuser not deciding at some point to seek help. Professional establishments are out there to help him, so there is no excuse for him not to get the help he needs.

As time passed, I continued to grow weary of my situation. I now know that this happens when we exhaust ourselves trying to find the answers. Ladies, the answer was there from the beginning of the relationship, from the moment we met each other, and from the moment we exchanged words and started dating.

Here's the thing: an abuser is on a mission from the time he approaches you. You are his victim. He chose you. In some cases, especially with the independence that some women have now, they may pursue men they have had their eye on, and may be running after the wrong type of person. Either way, the flashing yellow light to slow down is ignored or overlooked, along with all the red stoplights. When a red flag goes up, this is the time to stop, assess, make a 180-degree turn, and run. Do not walk but *run* away before the temptation gets too strong and you are knee deep in the middle of chaos.

> *"Watch and pray so that you will not fall into temptation. The spirit is willing, but the body is weak."*
> —*Matthew 26:41 (NIV)*

Personal Note: I point the finger at no one. I take full responsibility for entering such great darkness. I take full responsibility for ignoring every red flag that God placed in front of me. I believe He tried time and time again, and I ignored them time and time again. I believe in my heart that His grace and mercy continued to keep me throughout my ordeal, and it was His grace and mercy that eventually showed me a safe way to get out. Glory be to His name, for He is my deliverer.

CHAPTER FIVE

THE JOURNEY INSIGHT
(Self-Image)

It is sad when all a woman has to look forward to when she gets home, or when her abuser gets home, is some kind of confrontation that she must deal with again. Even at work, before she goes home, it is on her mind. The worry is constant and ongoing every day. The woman knows it is coming and she knows there is no way of escaping it. There is no way around it. In my past, I felt like the only thing to do was prepare for whatever type of abuse was coming.

The abuser expects you to just take the abuse and not dare try to strike back or form your lips to utter a word. Breaking the silence, depending on the situation, can be fatal. This is what the abuser wants you to do. This is what he thrives on. This is his reason to taunt you longer because you "stepped out of line" to defend yourself. I used to do this often only to regret it later. It took me a while to realize that it's not worth going tit for tat with someone who is mentally unstable. The reason why it took me so long to put my white flag up and become a silent partner is because my mom and four sisters were strong Black women. In my eyes they were fearless. They were tough. They fought women as well as the abusive men in their lives. Because of them, I have a voice, and whether my abuser liked it or not, I used my voice.

Did it make things worse for me? Yes, it did. But I was determined not to let him completely break me, and I was determined not to let him re-raise me. My mom and my sisters had already done that, and I made sure he knew it, so my struggle was hard. Later, I realized that choosing to be silent was the harder choice. There are probably many women, young and old, who suffer in silence and take every mean word and hit in silence, trying to block some of the blows to their body. This is truly a nightmare for many women around the world.

Insight (Self-Image)

Try to imagine the body of a woman being physically abused every day, not having a chance to heal from the beating from the prior day or the day before. Try to imagine her face (or your face) broken, swollen, and bleeding. Imagine the tears streaming down her face (your face) and trickling over the bumps and bruises. The tears sting and maybe even burn as they fall over the cuts on her face (your face).

Now let's focus on the body, which is also bruised. Her ribs (your ribs) ache with great pain, possibly broken. Her neck (your neck) has two handprints around it because he tried to cut off her breath (your breath) that God himself breathed into her being (your being). Try to imagine the bruises that are on her back (your back) from top to bottom. Dark unattractive marks that no one must ever see or know about. Imagine the pain deep inside of her (your) stomach or abdomen from being hit or kicked as she (you) lay on the floor in the fetal position. Imagine the only thought going through her mind (your mind) being whether he is going to go too far this time. *Will this finally be it, the end of the vicious nightmare?*

You do not know which time will be the last or which blow will be the one that will end your life. For me, I just wanted all the pain and suffering to come to an end. I became sick and tired of the constant drama behind closed doors. It is extremely sad when you prefer death over life because of your life's situation. I remember saying to myself, one of us has to die because we cannot live on this earth together. I could not get away from him because he refused to let me go. I literally found myself thinking of different ways to get this man out of my life. My way of thinking became very warped, dangerous, and scary.

CHAPTER SIX

A DESPERATE WOMAN

Desperate: moved by despair or utter loss of hope; showing a willingness to take any risk in order to change a bad or dangerous situation.

A desperate woman can become a dangerous woman when pushed to the point of no return. Meaning, she is at the end of her long, extended rope. A rope she has been clinging onto for many years. Men do not have a clue what a woman can really do when her mind, body, heart, and soul cannot take anymore. They do not know the things we contemplate when we are in a desperate, dying state. They do not know the kind of thoughts that enter a woman's mind out of hopelessness.

Not all women in an abusive relationship see themselves as weak and fragile. There are some who plan and scheme to get out of their situation. In my past situation, I began to think of things I had never thought of before. My thoughts were ungodly thoughts, and very unhealthy. Out of desperation, I considered deadly ways to strike back. It basically came down to two choices, my life or his.

Before I continue, I want to reflect on a movie called *The Burning Bed*. The movie premiered on NBC on October 8, 1984. It was based on a true story of Francine Hughes. The movie was about a couple who met, fell in love, and got married. Sometime after the marriage vows, the abuse hit her like a ton of bricks. It went from moderate to extreme in a very short time. The scene that was most disturbing was when she was dropped off at her mother's house. At this point, she was tired of the abuse. As she talked with her mom, she eventually told her she did not want to go back. She was basically pleading with her mom to let her stay. According to the movie, her mom told her "Some women have to put up with their men, especially if there are children. Mostly, the men don't mean it."

She went on to tell her, "You make a hard bed, you got to lay in it. It's not really so bad, is it?" I was not only in disbelief when I heard this, I was floored.

I could not comprehend how her mother, the person who should have her best interest at heart, would encourage her to stay in something that may eventually become fatal.

I can't imagine any family member or true friend, who claims to love me, giving me that kind of advice. That is a lie from the enemy (Satan). You do not have to stay with an abuser for the sake of the children. You have a right to get yourself and your children out of that dangerous situation. You have a right to separate yourself from being tormented and beaten and the right to shield your children from being in a toxic environment. Beware of people, including family and friends, who give you deadly advice, especially since they are not living in your nightmare. If they have never experienced abuse in any form or aren't an expert in the matter, they cannot give you advice or tell you the right thing to do. Those are the kind of people you need to distance yourself from because they do not have your best interest at heart. Remove them as fast as possible, so you can focus on hearing the voice of God. He will not lead you astray. He will remove all stumbling blocks that are hindering you from getting to a safe place.

Some years back, I visited a church and the message was amazing. What stuck with me most about the pastor's message was when he said, "The very thing that God is trying to separate, we are trying to keep together. We need to pay close attention to what God is telling us to do, not what society is telling us to do." It is extremely important to listen to God-given advice. The wrong advice will leave you feeling empty and desperate, and desperation can lead you in the wrong direction.

Some of us reach a point of being tired of being abused, dumped on, trampled on, and being hurt—mentally, physically, and emotionally. Some of us can no longer shed a tear because the tears have dried up, and the love we had in our hearts for our significant other has been replaced with bitterness, resentment, and the worst kind of hate. I knew I was beyond rational thinking and had ventured into an unnatural state of mind because I was so consumed with an all-consuming hate. I found myself in the red zone and did not know how to get out of it. The thing is, I did not care. All I wanted was to inflict pain and suffering on the one who was hurting me, or take him completely out, so I could be free from bondage. My reality was that he was my enemy because a man who truly loved me certainly could not be capable of inflicting pain and suffering upon me on purpose. There is no excuse for a man to ever verbally tear a woman down or put his hands on her in a harmful way. No excuse at all.

At some point in the relationship, I got to the point of no return. God showed up, and He showed me a safe way to get out without harming my abuser. As a child of God, I knew that God breathed life into my being, and He is the only one who has the power to take it away. I was not proud of how I got away from my abuser, but I was blessed that I got away with my life, and with no vengeance in my heart. There was much fear, but no vengeance.

> *Do not repay anyone evil for evil.*
> *Be careful to do what is right in the eyes of everybody. Do not take revenge my friends, but leave room for God's wrath, for it is written: "It is mine to avenge; I will repay," says the Lord.*
> *—Romans 12:17, 19 (NIV)*

At this point in my testimony, I would like to give honor to my mom who stayed by my side the entire time, while I planned my escape. When I got a chance to see her, I could see the worry and pain she had in her eyes for me. I feel like I'd put her through so much. My mom tried with all her heart to warn me in the beginning, but I ignored her intuition. My mom had married at a young age. I was told it was an arranged marriage, and the man who became her husband, also became her abuser. She suffered greatly in that marriage and she, like me, had to plan and sneak away with the help of her uncle and a family friend. They bought her and her children a one-way bus ticket to Phoenix, Arizona.

When you think there is no way out, God will make a way. I believe my mom recognized something in my abuser that I could not see. Maybe it was immaturity and ignorance on my part. I had no experience being in a relationship, and since I failed to heed her warning, I suffered greatly. Moms know more than we could ever imagine. Especially when they have been there and done that. When your parents are telling you the *right* thing to do, do not ignore it. Good parents are looking out for your best interest.

As far back as I can remember, in the neighborhoods I grew up in, there was often some kind of abuse. From women being beaten by their boyfriends/spouse, to gang abuse or children being abused by their parents.

Sometimes the abuse was overwhelming to listen to, and overwhelming to watch outside my home. Inside my home there were times when my older siblings did not get along. As a little girl, I walked around with so much fear inside because of the violence I grew up around. I did not know how to deal with fear, so I tucked it away and moved on with my life. I did not think that kind of fear would ever surface again, but it did, and it almost cost me my life.

We have two choices, enter the red flag zone or walk away from it. The key is paying attention to the warning signs, being attentive to the voice of God, and not second-guessing what He is telling you to do. Just do it. Before I continue, I want to share some verses from Psalm 118 with you. This is my favorite Psalm because God carried me through it all and He never let the enemy take me completely out.

PSALM 118 *(NIV)*

1. Give thanks to the Lord, for he is good; his love endures forever.

2. When hard pressed, I cried to the Lord; he brought me into a spacious place.

3. The Lord is with me; I will not be afraid.

4. What can mere mortals do to me?

5. The Lord is with me; he is my helper. I look in triumph on my enemies.

6. I was pushed back and about to fall, but the Lord helped me.

7. The Lord is my strength and my defense; he has become my salvation.

8. I will not die but live, and will proclaim what the Lord has done.

9. The Lord has chastened me severely, but he has not given me over to death.

I realize now that God never left my side. He gave me the strength I needed to get through some of my weakest and most fragile moments. When I felt as though I could not take another step, it was then that he picked me up and carried me the rest of the way. There were many, many times I did not want to go on. I was desperate, broken, and did not care to be fixed. Because of the love God has for me, I believe He wanted more for me than I wanted for myself. He watched me go through it all, and I believe He suffered through it with me. It must have grieved His spirit to watch one of His children, whom He loves so passionately and unconditionally, go through such a tragic season. The thing is, I had to go through it. Why? Because I chose not to take heed to the warning signs. I chose not to listen to the voice of God. I chose to ignore my mom's concern about the relationship. My suffering was inevitable because I chose to do my own thing. I chose to stray off the road, the path that God had for me. I chose to follow a man, instead of my Creator. I chose to fear a man more than my Creator. When I chose that, I chose death. I gave up on life.

Do not be anxious about anything, but in every situation, by prayer and petition, with thanksgiving, present your requests to God.
—Philippians 4:6 (NIV)

I became a prisoner to the sin that had me bound. I was more than knee deep in sin because I chose to live with a man I was not married to for years, and I chose to continue in the relationship when I knew my abuser had some serious issues. This brings me to a familiar scripture that I have read repeatedly. At first, I did not understand it so I made my request known to God. In return, He gave me the wisdom to understand its meaning. I struggled with the same problem the Apostle Paul had.

> *I do not understand what I do. For what I want to do I do not do, but what I hate I do. And if I do what I do not want to do, I agree that the law is good. As it is, it is no longer I myself who do it, but it is sin living in me. For I know that sin itself does not dwell in me, that is, in my sinful nature. For I have the desire to do what is good, but I cannot carry it out. For I do not do the good I want to do, but the evil I do not want to do—this I keep on doing. Now if I do what I do not want to do, it is no longer I who do it, but it is sin living in me that does it. (Romans 7:15-20 NIV)*

I found myself time after time doing the thing I hated the most and not knowing why I kept doing it. Like the Apostle Paul, what I wanted to do, I did not do. Even though I grew to know it was wrong. I knew it was wrong for me to stay in the mess I was in. Every time I tried to flee the situation, I found myself right back in it, only to regret it later. It was a sick cycle, and I did not know how to free myself from it. I did not know that I could make it in this world without my abuser. Insecurity became my best friend, and the fact that he would come looking for me, and succeeded in finding me, did not help either. I constantly found myself in a no-win situation. Therefore, I gave up on hope and walked away from faith. I laid down my white flag and surrendered to the enemy. Thanks be to my Lord and Savior, Jesus Christ, because He had other plans for me and delivered me out of the darkness. It took some time for me to move on, but I did move on. The next step was to learn how to love myself and trust that I would be able to make better choices as I moved forward.

CHAPTER SEVEN

SELF-LOVE

Most of my life I was taught in the home or in the church to cater to other people's needs. "Be helpful whenever you can," "Be giving, don't be selfish," "Think about the needs of others," someone would say to me at one time or another. I have lived my life according to this guidance, and as I grew older, I catered more to everyone else's wants and needs and forgot about the plans and needs I had for myself.

When I met my abuser, I was sixteen years old. I was not exactly full of life. I was still trying to figure out life. I had hopes and dreams, and they included a career, a husband, and children. As time and years went on, I put everything I dreamed of doing on hold and began to focus on what my abuser wanted out of life. As I grew to love him, what he wanted and the dream he was pursuing at the time became increasingly important to me. I simply threw all my plans out the window and closed it, only to regret it later.

I did not know how to be a selfish person. I grew up in a very unselfish household. Besides myself, there were six other children, and then my youngest brother came later. I remember having to share toys, beds, and clothing. I do not remember any of my older siblings having selfish ways. If my family could have fed the whole neighborhood, believe me, it would have been done.

There is nothing wrong with catering to the wants, needs, and dreams of others, just do not forget to include your needs as well. Self-love is so important. What you want and need out of life is just as important as what other people want and need out of life. I know now that what I wanted out of life should have been the first thing on my list. It should have been my top priority. This may sound selfish, but it is true. Not only did I not know how to love myself enough to walk away from the danger I saw coming my way, but I also did not know how to have respect for myself and demand that others respect me as well. I had no clue about who I was. I would understand later that just as I can see that vulnerability in my younger self now, the enemy could spot it in me then.

What Does Self-Love Mean?

Self-love is being able to start with you first. We are to love others as we love ourselves. We must value who we are as individuals and know our self-worth. When you come to know who you really are and know God's purpose for your life, there will be no compromise. The enemy will not be able to slip in. At sixteen I had no idea what self-love meant and there are probably millions of people in the world who do not know what it means either. As life goes on, and time passes by, we tend to get caught up in what we should do, what we can do, and what we need to be to everyone else except ourselves, and before you know it, like in my own life, many wasted years pass by. Instead of learning from the lesson you thought you graduated from, you unknowingly start the cycle all over again. I became a servant to the needs of others. There is nothing wrong with serving and loving others. There is nothing wrong with wanting to see someone else succeed in what they truly believe in—as long as you do not exclude yourself. I cannot stress it enough. Do not forget about you. You are important.

When you truly love yourself, it will keep you out of harm's way because you are going to think enough of yourself to take the needed time out to find a quiet place where you can sit down, pray, and ask the Holy Spirit to help you decipher whether you should move forward or completely end whatever you are facing that may be a danger to you mentally, emotionally, and/or physically. The most important thing to do is not lose focus and stay on the path God has set for you.

"For I know the plans I have for you." declares the LORD, "plans to prosper you and not to harm you, plans to give you hope and a future."
—*Jeremiah 29:11 (NIV).*

God wants what is best for us, and if He wants the best, we should also want the best. To have the best that life has to offer, you have to know who you really are as a woman. You must stand firm in your beliefs and the goals you have for yourself. Never compromise your morals and values for anyone. Most importantly, know that you are a complete woman in Christ. There are so many women who believe they are incomplete without a man, and that is another lie from the pit of hell. You do not need a man in your life to be whole. When God created you from the rib he took from Adam, and breathed the breath of life in you, you were complete, lacking nothing. When you are confident in who you are, it will be extremely hard for a man who is needy with low self-esteem and who does not know who he is in Christ, to bring you into the dark world he lives in. When a man and a woman come before God in holy matrimony, they are two whole people becoming one flesh in Christ. Half of a man and half of a woman make out to be a complete mess, and the relationship will eventually take a turn for the worse. This turn for the worse happens because both spouses are looking for the other to complete them, and that is impossible. Only God can make you whole.

Do not sell yourself short by entering a relationship with your tank half-filled. Do not violate the standards you have for yourself because if you violate one, you will slowly continue to do it until all have been completely broken. Compromise is a good thing when used in the right way and in a healthy dynamic. But if you're the only one compromising, you should re-evaluate the situation.

God gives us one precious life to live on this earth. My cry out to every woman is to choose wisely. Guard your heart, mind, and soul because the enemy wants them all.

Self-Love (Part Two)
Written by: My Youngest Daughter at age 11
January 13, 2000

Self-Love Ought to Come First

It's been said, and it's true, that falling in love isn't about finding the right person but being the right person. And the judgment about how right you are must come from you, and not your intended. If you really like yourself, it's most likely that you'll fall in love, for the positivity that you feel in yourself becomes a lot easier to share with many of the people you meet.

Whatever you find about yourself that you don't like will eventually come out in one of the conversations that you have with your spouse.

Either way it goes, if you love your spouse more than you love yourself, your relationship will be sure to fail.

A lady named Christine went through a lot of abusive men. They were abusive to her because she didn't love herself enough to tell them to leave her alone, so she just let them beat her until they left.

The question is, if self-love is so important for both personal survival and developing loving relationships, why do so few people seem to have it?

And how do people develop it?

This affects me because as other people and I read and listen to this, we have to grow up trying to love ourselves and try to make sure that we don't end up getting with abusive people.

If I could change one thing about people getting abused it would be to make sure that the people who are getting abused get out of that type of relationship and stay out of it.

The day I found my daughter's class report and the subject she chose to write about at such a young age hit me like a ton of bricks, so I decided to take a break from organizing old paperwork. I sat down and read it, and the tears started flowing. They were coming down like rain. It broke me to my core because she never should have been raised in that type of environment. My oldest daughter was also affected by it. It broke my heart that out of all the things to write about in the world, especially at age eleven, she chose to write about self-love and attaching abuse along with it. I have read it many times since then and sometimes I wondered if the lady in her report is me. Then it dawned on me that it could not be because she mentioned that the lady, Christine, had gone through a lot of abusive men, and I had only one experience. I believe this is when I knew I had to exit the nightmare.

Years later, I continued to grieve over the fact that I kept my beautiful daughters, the two people I love and cherish with everything in me, and more than anyone on this earth, in an atmosphere they should have never experienced or been exposed to. I regret it even more because it impacted their lives in many ways from childhood to adulthood. It has not only been a healing journey for me, but also for them. If only I could do it all over again and erase what has been done, but I cannot. The only person I blame for their misfortune is myself, and that will go to the grave with me.

This is why it is so imperative that we pay close attention to the warning signs of an abusive predator and not play around with it or entertain it as a thought, because you will not win. If you do move forward despite what your intuition is telling you, there will be consequences, not only for you, but for the children you decide to bring into this world that belong to him also. You must think beyond yourself. Visualize the big picture and ask God to reveal to you where the hidden danger lies in the man you are interested in. When you ask, be sure to patiently wait for your answer. If He reveals to you any red flags, my advice is not to walk away but run.

No temptation has seized you except what is common to man. And God is faithful; he will not let you be tempted, beyond what you can bear. But when you are tempted, he will also provide a way out.
—1 Corinthians 10:13 (NIV)

Let no one say when he is tempted, "I am tempted by God;" for God cannot be tempted by evil, nor does He Himself tempt anyone. But each one is tempted when he is drawn away by his own desires and enticed.
—James 1:13-14 (NKJV)

Submit yourselves therefore to God. Resist the devil, and he will flee from you.
—James 4:7 (KJV)

Chapter Eight

KNOW WHO YOU ARE

It is imperative to know who you are. Your heart and mind need to be on the same page. Do not let one override the other because this will leave you confused about which one to listen to and you may end up making a costly decision.

Stand strong on the goals and the path you have laid out for yourself. Have a made-up mind that the only person who is authorized to change and redirect your path is God. Always include Him in every decision you make, and He will direct your path. Be confident enough to know that if you must, you will make it in this world with or without a man by your side. Also, make up your mind to be truly happy with or without a man in your life. This is what my oldest daughter would tell me every so often when I was feeling down. She would say,

"Mom, happiness is a choice." She was right. It is a personal choice to be happy. Make sure you choose your friends wisely. It makes a big difference when you surround yourself with people who are go-getters, people who are confident and comfortable being who they are, and people who support the goals you are aiming to reach. This also includes the man with whom you become romantically involved. Make sure you distance yourself from anyone who sets off internal alarms. Listen to your body and be mindful of the physiological responses like discomfort, increased heart rate (for negative reasons), anxiety, etc. Stay away from men who try to diminish your goals and dreams with sentiments of "you can't" or "you won't." Do not think twice about it, just walk away. Also, do not worry about what will be said after your exit. It is not important. Keep in mind who you are and what you stand for.

You cannot afford to be confused about anything concerning you because that is how the enemy (an abuser) gets in and slowly changes your plan to align only with his. Then, it goes downward from there because if he can detect one area of vulnerability, it gives him something to latch onto. It gives the enemy an opportunity to slip in and start to break down your image of self and create a new image where he is in control. We only have one life, so please do not allow the enemy to get in and destroy it. Choose life.

I am a Christian woman and the God I serve has brought me through many storms. There has always been someone I could not physically see, but He was there. Sometimes I can feel a presence in the room with me. I'll look back to see if someone is there, and in those instances, I believe it is a spirit with me, but I just cannot see it in the natural realm. I know with everything inside of me that God is real, and He will make himself known to you if you seek Him with a sincere heart. I truly believe in the power of prayer because prayer changes things, but you must have faith.

I tell you the truth, if you have faith as small as a mustard seed, you can say to this mountain, 'move from here to there' and it will move. Nothing will be impossible for you.
—*Matthew 17:20 (NIV)*

My mountain was moved many years ago, but it has taken me almost a lifetime to get in touch with who I really am and to know that I am someone special. I am fearfully and wonderfully made by God, and for His purpose. I deserve the best that life has to offer, and nothing less. Therefore, I owe no man my life. I do not have to stay in an abusive relationship. I do not have to spend the rest of my life being miserable and unhappy. I do not have to spend the rest of my life waddling in self-pity. Also, I do not have to spend the rest of my life moaning and crying or contemplating suicide because I am at the end of my rope and afraid to do what is right. It came down to two choices: let go or climb back up. I chose life.

CHAPTER NINE

RECONSTRUCTION

Now that you have come up out of the darkness, it is time to move on. This is not going to be an easy task. It will be one of the hardest things you will ever have to do. Everything is new, and though you may think you are out there all by yourself, you are not. God is on this journey with you. Once again, you will be the one who will make every major decision for your life and/or the life of your children. For me, it was an extremely scary thought. It was my first time being in a home that felt like my own. Along with my youngest daughter, we moved into my first apartment. Before that moment, I'd gone from my parents' house and their rules to my boyfriend's/husband's house and his rules.

After I finally left, I felt fear, then a sense of emptiness because I did not know where to start.

There were many days and nights of crying uncontrollably. I cried even when I did not feel like crying. But I had to cry it all out. It was a cleansing process. A grieving-for-me process because I had been dead for so long. Crying is a must. It begins the healing process. It soothes your soul and empties out the pain you feel inside, little by little. You cannot move forward holding on to the past. Let go and let the healing begin.

As you continue to move forward, the next phase in the healing process is to release all bitterness, anger, and resentment. Leave behind every dark memory because this will always leave you in a depressed state. If you must think of something from the relationship, let it be the brief and rare times when you did get along or a time when you shared laughter together. Laughter is also a healing agent. Try to laugh often as it relieves heaviness and makes the load you are carrying a little lighter. I have heard it said many times before that laughter is the best medicine.

If possible, refrain from watching movies with sad and depressing endings. This includes movies about abuse in any form during the healing process because at some point, it is going to trigger a bad memory and send you soaring backwards (I have been there and done that). Do not allow negative thoughts to rise and overshadow you. God gives us the power to rebuke the enemy and take charge of our thoughts. This will be the most difficult one of all, but it can be accomplished through prayer.

I can do all things through Christ who strengthens me.
—Philippians 4:13 (KJV)

Moving forward means there are some things in your life you are going to have to prioritize. "Love the Lord your God with all your heart and with all your soul and with all your mind and with all your strength. The second is this: 'Love your neighbor as yourself.' There is no commandment greater than these." (Mark 12:30-31 NIV)

I believe it is impossible to love your neighbor if you do not know how to love yourself. Loving and caring about your well-being means no compromise of any kind, especially if it does not line up with the word of God, and if it is out of His will concerning you. It is vital that you get to know yourself. Get a piece of paper and write down the areas where you are strong, as well as the areas where you are weak.

This will help you focus and build on the vulnerable areas in your life so you're less likely to repeat the same mistake.

You are powerful, so be confident about every decision you will make concerning your life going forward. Identify the goals you will set for yourself and what you will and will not accept. Be strong enough to demand respect in every way. It doesn't matter who you are demanding it from as long as you demand your respect.

The good news is that there is a whole new life out there waiting for you! A world you became unfamiliar with, but this time around, you hold the pencil, and what stands before you is a huge piece of construction paper. Your job is to reconstruct your life, which means to sketch out, build on, re-form, and put together a positive roadmap for yourself. As you do, don't forget to include God throughout the entire process. Pray every step of the way that your path going forward will be His will and not your own. This is not going to be an overnight project because rebuilding is a lifelong process with stumbling blocks along the way. How big or how small these blocks are lies within your hands. Be careful how you handle some of your stumbling blocks. Do not allow them to become a deterrent. Do not turn them into mountains. You have the power to move them out of your way. Take some time out to pray and seek God's guidance because you may have to go in a different direction, and God is the only one who can get you there.

Now, before heading out on this new adventure, you will need to do one thing, because this is something that, once again, you cannot do all by yourself. It takes a higher being (God), not a human being, to help you fight and conquer situations as they arise while you are on your journey back to life. I cannot stress enough that God is the only one who can guide you in the direction you really need to go. Trust Him with everything in you and believe He is with you and covering you every step of the way.

Trust me when I say, do not put your faith in the hands of friends and family because there will be many that give advice, but if they have not been where you came from, they cannot direct you toward the right path. Also, be aware that some of the mutual friends you and your abuser shared may turn their backs on you. They may turn against you because your abuser also has a story to tell, it just may not be an accurate one. The loyalty of mutual friends may remain with him because those friends may not desire to understand the truth. Do not let it be a stumbling block for you. Guard your heart and keep moving forward.

I can honestly say, with all my heart and soul, that from the beginning of my ordeal until the end, and then some, God never left my side. He truly brought me through some trying times.

> *Be strong and courageous. Do not be afraid; do not be discouraged, for the Lord your God will be with you wherever you go.*
> *—Joshua 1:9 (Zondervan NIV)*

At some point a little further down the line, you will find the reconstructing course is not as bad as you thought it would be. It just takes time, and time is good, especially for the healing process. In the meantime, focus on things you always wanted to do, or you were not allowed to do. Make a bucket list of things that are fun, exciting, and life-changing. Dare to do things you have never done before. There is an entire world out there. Take time to travel and experience it. Live each day as if it were your last.

Eventually, a season or two down the line, or

sooner for some, the thought of dating may be an option again. When that time comes, do not judge every man according to the one you had to flee from. That was my biggest problem. I remained bitter and angry for a considerable amount of time and ended up judging every man I met based on the past. I saw them all as the same. I did not want to give any of them a chance. It got to a point where I didn't even want them to look at me. I also did not want any man to part his lips to speak to me. I did not want to have to look men in the eyes. My thought process was that they are useless, and I wondered why they were created to be a part of humanity. I felt as if they were a waste of flesh. I honestly had it bad. I was a walking, broken mess for a tremendous amount of time.

At some point, I realized I could not walk around carrying so much resentment because it would eventually kill me. The truth is that I was just as angry and bitter with myself for allowing fear, insecurity, and low self-esteem to keep me in such a dark and dangerous place.

Throughout my healing process, I had to do a great deal of soul searching, praying, repenting, forgiving, and crying. I did all this over and over again. Not only did I have to forgive my abuser, but I also had to forgive myself, which took a great deal of time. I have often heard that forgiveness is not for the one who hurt you, but for you. Initially, I did not understand that statement, but the meaning of it was revealed to me when I heard it in a message at church. Forgiveness brings freedom. The bondage of unforgiveness is completely destructive. When you forgive, you are no longer carrying the past around on your shoulders. The power the enemy had over you is broken. You cannot move forward with unforgiveness in your heart, not even towards yourself. It took some doing, but I did empty the unforgiveness out.

> *Create in me a clean heart,*
> *O God; and renew a right spirit within me.*
> —*Psalm 51:10 (KJV)*

As time moved on, I began to feel comfortable around men again, and there were times I missed holding hands and being held in the arms of a man. I felt this way because the flesh does get weak at times. When this happens, the only thing to do is pray and ask God to deliver you from those feelings.

As for me, I kept a safe distance from men because I was still dealing with trust issues. Also, because I knew in my heart I was not quite ready yet. On the positive side, I did learn from my mistakes and understood how to guard my heart more, as well as pay close attention to warning signs. I decided, for the second time around, if it came, that settling would not be an option. Settling would not even be a thought. I knew what I wanted in a man. I knew all the do's and don'ts. I demanded my respect because I did not have time for flashbacks, foolishness, or things that were not true or honest. Life is too short to live in a deep, dark cave waddling in self-pity. It is time for women to rise, come up out of the darkness, and go into the marvelous light of life.

The Power to Rise Up is in Our Hands!

Chapter Ten

WORDS OF WISDOM

Don't

Don't ever think you're a nobody.

Don't ever think a man will make you whole.

Don't ever let anyone take control over your life.

Don't ever rush into any relationship.

Don't ever ignore the signs of abuse.

Don't ever ignore what your self-consciousness is telling you.

Don't ever give up your dreams or your goals for any man.

Don't ever lead a life that is a lie.

Don't ever think your happiness is not important.

Don't ever think there is no way out.

Believe

There is always a light at the end of the tunnel, just believe.

Believe you are a precious gift from God given to Man.

Believe you can do all things you set your mind to do.

Believe you deserve to have the best life has to offer.

Believe you should not walk behind any man. You came from his side, not his back.

Believe you owe it to yourself to be the best you can be.

Believe self-love is very important.

Believe self-respect is a must and should always come first.

Believe you deserve to be in a healthy, happy, peaceful, and fearless relationship.

Believe the power of prayer can break all strongholds.

Believe there is a way out of every dark situation.

Believe in You when no one else does.

Just Believe!

Scriptures for Additional Reading

There is no fear in love. But perfect love drives out fear, because fear has to do with punishment. The one who fears is not made perfect in love.

1 John 4:18

So do not Fear, for I am with you; do not be dismayed, for I am your God. I will strengthen you and help you; I will uphold you with my righteous right hand.

Isaiah 41:10

For the Lord your God is the one who goes with you to fight for you against your enemies to give you victory.

Deuteronomy 20:4

When I am afraid, I will trust in you.

Psalm 56:3

Be strong and courageous. Do not be afraid or terrified because of them, for the Lord your God goes with you; he will never leave you nor forsake you.

Deuteronomy 31:6

Cast your cares on the Lord and he will sustain you; he will never let the righteous fall.

Psalm 55:22

But those who hope in the Lord will renew their strength. They will soar on wings like eagles; they will run, and not grow weary, they will walk and not be faint.

Isaiah 40:31

If God is for us, who can be against us.

Romans 8:31

All scriptures are from the New International Version.

About the Author

As an advocate for women who have experienced abuse, Veronica Riley is purposed and graced to obediently execute God's calling over her life, which includes the philosophy that we should never stop learning because staying informed may save a life and create a new and improved path in one's journey. Veronica believes her powerful testimony about the ordeal she experienced and survived can help women of all ages avoid being in harmful romantic relationships. The Arizona native is a loving and faithful wife and mother of two beautiful daughters.

www.ingramcontent.com/pod-product-compliance
Lightning Source LLC
Chambersburg PA
CBHW031445120626
46545CB00006B/2560